M000121179

Laurie, a marine geologist, has traveled extensively from the Arctic Circle to Saipan and beyond, conducting geophysical surveys. She has mapped thousands of kilometers by plane, boat, and foot. She has written *A Young Person's Field Guide to Finding Lost Shipwrecks* for her love of science and for the essential need for children to find a connection to themselves through math and science.

Laurie is a member of EAGE (Women in Geoscience and Engineering) and AGU (American Geophysical Union), and is a firm believer in giving back to the community by doing what you love. This is her first book.

To my daughter, Emily, who is more of a treasure than any shipwreck could ever hold.

Laurie Anne Zaleski

A YOUNG PERSON'S FIELD GUIDE TO FINDING LOST SHIPWRECKS

The Search for the Santisima

AUSTIN MACAULEY PUBLISHERS™

LONDON • CAMBRIDGE • NEW YORK • SHARJAH

Copyright © Laurie Anne Zaleski (2020)

Ordering Information:
Quantity sales: special discounts are available on quantity purchases by corporations, associations, and others. For details, contact the publisher at the address below.

Publisher's Cataloging-in-Publication data
Zaleski, Laurie Anne
A Young Person's Field Guide to Finding Lost Shipwrecks

ISBN 9781643789019 (Paperback)
ISBN 9781643789026 (Hardback)
ISBN 9781645365556 (ePub e-book)

Library of Congress Control Number: 2019916884

www.austinmacauley.com/us

First Published (2020)
Austin Macauley Publishers LLC
40 Wall Street, 28th Floor
New York, NY 10005
USA

mail-usa@austinmacauley.com
+1 (646) 5125767

With grateful acknowledgment to the following:

Susan Wilson for knowing the right person. Dee Brown for being the right person.

My friends and readers for their unwavering support and enthusiasm.

The crew of the *Hercules*. We started as mates and became friends. Michelle for being the best intern ever.

RPMNF for their continuous commitment to advancing maritime archeology and bringing history to the surface.

Thank you to RPMNF and the expedition team for permission to share the tale.

Table of Contents

Chapter 1

Trouble on the Bridge

Crud! The computer on the bridge is not working; I am looking at a black screen when I should be looking at a map, a nautical chart to be exact. There is little solace in that the screen is black and not blue. Black is better than blue. As you may guess a 'Blue Screen of Death' is not a good thing. Luckily, the computer broke while we are still at dock. It's easier to fix things when we're at dock and the nearest electronics store is only a car ride, not a boat ride away. Besides, things get bumpy when you're at sea.

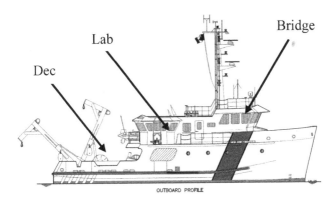

Blueprint of a Research Vessel (R/V)

Downstairs on the computer in the lab, I clearly see a chart of Cadiz, Spain with a series of parallel lines drawn along the coast. These lines make up a survey block. This particular survey block is where we will be exploring in hopes of finding a shipwreck. And not just any shipwreck, we are looking for the *Santisima*, the greatest warship of its time, which sunk in 1805 during the Battle of Trafalgar.

The captain should see the same map on his screen that I am looking at in the lab. He doesn't. We can't leave the dock until he does. All the systems need to be up and running. Precious time is ticking away. We only have the summer to work, when the weather is good, so let the troubleshooting begin.

I hope it's the monitor that's broken because if not, it's the cable. Changing a monitor is easy, but rewiring 100 meters of cable, about the length of city block, through the floor and walls of a boat is not fun. Being petite helps when working on a boat because you fit into tiny nooks and crannies. I am not a small person, but luckily Michelle is. Lucky for me that is, not so lucky for Michelle, as that means she does a lot of crawling through cramped spaces. She wears a bandana so bugs don't get in her hair.

What it's like to run cable on a boat.

After some trial and error, we cross our fingers as I power up the monitor with a quick flick. There is a green flash as it turns on, so far so good. After a few clicks and whirls – success. It's working. Fantastic, we can soon be underway.

Chapter 2

The Expedition

My name is Laurie. I am a marine geologist and work with maritime archeologists. Maritime archeology is a specialized branch of archeology, which studies the physical remains of human interaction with a water body. Simply put, we look for and study remains of things that have sunk or have been submerged underwater over time: sunken vessels, human remains, and submerged landscapes to name a few. I am all good with the sunken vessels and landscapes, the human remains part makes me a little squeamish.

I was the survey manager on the expedition in search of the *Santisima Trinidad* and the *Argonauta*, two ships from the Battle of Trafalgar. Our job was to find and photograph any remains of the wrecks which sunk off the coast of Spain over two hundred years ago. The various systems used during the expedition include multibeam and side-scan sonars, magnetometers, and an ROV (Remotely Operated Vehicle). All this and SCUBA (Self Contained Underwater Breathing Apparatus) divers too.

We (myself along with three archeologists, two university students on a summer internship, three captains, one cook, one engineer, two scuba divers, and one able-bodied seaman) are aboard the *R/V Hercules*, a 37-meter research vessel and in the midst of preparing for the upcoming expedition. There are boxes of equipment, cables, and tools scattered throughout the ship and a whirl of activity as final preparations are made on *Hercules* for its maiden voyage as a Research Vessel.

The team comes from all walks of life: archeologists with PhDs, me with a master's degree in geological oceanography, students who are still in college on a summer internship, vessel engineers, boat captains, deck hands, scuba divers, and cooks. Everyone has a role to play on the team, whether it's making sure we have good food to eat, driving the boat safely, deciding the search area, or keeping the deck of the *Hercules* clean and hazard free; we are all important to the success of the expedition. We all do have one thing in common though – an adventuring spirit.

What team will you play on when you grow up? What adventures are in your future? The answer is as vast as the bottom of the sea and yours to discover.

Chapter 3

Mission Seemingly Impossible

To find a shipwreck, there is a lot to put together ahead of time. First off, you need to know what you are looking for. Are you looking for any shipwreck, lots of shipwrecks or are you looking for a specific ship? The answer to this question directs where your research begins. For this expedition, we are looking for a known shipwreck, the *Santisima*.

Once archeologists know what they are looking for, they spend a lot of time researching.

They ask the six questions all investigators ask – who, what, where, when, why, and how. Where was the ship going? Who was the captain? When did it sink? Why was the ship there? How did it sink? Even weather patterns are important. Is this an area that's usually stormy? Which way does the wind blow? Can you think of a few more questions that you would ask if you were looking for a sunken ship?

To answer these questions about the *Santisima*, our archeologist, Dr. Jeff starts in the library months before *Hercules* and the crew arrive in Cadiz. He reads old, old papers called historical documents to learn as much as he could about the Battle of Trafalgar. He follows the trail of captains and their vessels. Ship ledgers along with any recent studies about the ship and area provide additional information that help the investigation.

Example of a historical document

After learning about the past, Jeff looks to the present. He travels to Cadiz, Spain. He meets and talks with local fishermen. Fish love to swim around shipwrecks because wrecks provide a plentiful food source and protection from predators, so if there's a lot of fish in one spot it may be where a ship has sunk. What's pulled up in nets and what's washed ashore also provide important clues to the mysteries under the sea. Stories get bigger as the afternoon sun gets smaller.

He listens to stories handed down through the generations, from grandfathers to fathers to sons – the whereabouts of treasure recounted over wine and tapas. Fish tales are told as they argue and debate into the night.

Jeff records many stories which he will catalog and review in the morning. He enjoys his fill of tapas, small plates of different foods, snacking on octopus, jamón, and other delicacies of Cadiz. He thinks his Spanish has improved throughout the night. It hasn't.

Jeff returns to the office and is happy with all the information he gathered and is feeling positive about the expedition. There is a myriad of reasons why ships sink. Doing thorough research ahead of time saves a lot of time and money. Learning about the battle from historical records and local folklore has given him vital clues as to where the ship may be now. Remember, it was a ship before it was a shipwreck.

Based on what archeologists learn from their research, they make the best guess – a hypothesis – about where the ship could be. This area can be very large or very small, like when you lose your backpack. If you know you left it at school, you know where to start to look. If you have no idea where it is, it could be any number of places – your room, the car, at school, on the bus, and so on. Your search area is much larger with less information. And this is for sure – if you look in the wrong spot, you will never find what it is you're looking for. Now imagine it's not your backpack, you just heard about someone losing a backpack years ago... and it's under water. Welcome to my world!

Chapter 4

Battle at Sea

We are looking for the two ships from the Battle of Trafalgar – the *Santisima Trinidad* and the *Argonauta*. This was the final battle between the British and the combined forces of the Spanish and French. Long, ongoing hostilities between the two began in the West Indies, an ocean away. The battle of Trafalgar took place off the coast of Spain at Cape Trafalgar on October 21, 1805.

Distance between West Indies and Cape Trafalgar

The British fleet was made up of thirty-two ships led by Admiral Lord Nelson and Vice Admiral Collingwood. The British navy was considered the best in the world at the time, much more experienced than their French or Spanish equivalents.

The French had twenty-three ships and the Spanish fifteen; a combined fleet of thirty-eight ships. Admiral Villeneuve commanded the French fleet and Admirals D'Aliva and Cisternas the Spanish.

By October 7th, the British fleet was fully assembled and anchored near the Strait of Gibraltar, over the horizon and out of sight of their enemy. The Franco-Spanish fleet was at port in Cadiz. Small, fast ships called frigates, relayed the movements of the Franco-Spanish to Lord Nelson.

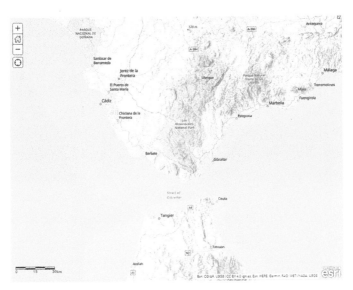

Map of Cadiz, Cape Trafalgar, Strait of Gibraltar

On October 18, 1805 Admiral Villeneuve gave the order to leave port in pursuit of the British. Because of light winds only twelve ships were able to set sail from Cadiz on the morning of 19th of October. By October 20th, the light winds of the 18th had strengthened and stormy weather ensued. The British fleet spent the day in the strait, while the combined French Spanish fleet was en route to the Strait of Gibraltar.

The Battle of Trafalgar by Montague Dawson

In the early morning of 21st of October, the two enemies crossed paths at Cape Trafalgar and the final battle began. By the end of the day, after hours of brutal fighting, the British devastated the enemy fleet, destroying 19 of their 23 ships. 4,800 men were dead and 3,700 wounded. Lord Nelson, commander of the British fleet and Britain's national hero was among the dead. His death was mourned throughout the British Empire.

The *Argonauta*, an 80-gun Spanish ship, was the first ship to surrender, surrendering to the British ship, *Belleisle*. The *Santisima Trinidad* was Britain's biggest prize of the battle, the greatest sailing ship of its era. With four decks and 136 guns, it was the Spanish flagship, and the last ship to surrender.

After the French and Spanish surrendered, the British had over fifty ships in tow on their way back to England, half of them demasted. Demasted means that they had no sails. The ongoing bad weather during the battle worsened into a storm, rising into a hurricane, which blew for seven days straight. The storm along with the instability of the ships in tow caused many of them to go out of control, drifting onto rocks near the shore and breaking up.

Both the *Santisima* and the *Argonauta* were scuttled, sunk on purpose, on the orders of Admiral Collingwood who took command after the passing of Lord Nelson. Records state that the *Santisima* went down between 7 and 8 leagues, 21 to 24 miles south of Cadiz.

We begin at a dock in Cadiz, Spain.

Chapter 5

All Aboard

It is May 1st and the *Hercules* is at dock at the Port Du Cadiz. The expedition team has just arrived and settling in aboard the *Hercules*. The *Hercules* was shipped from the RPM Nautical Foundation's office in Florida to Spain by boat. Funny, right? A boat being shipped by boat.

A very large heavy lift ship cradled the *Hercules* along with many other ships and sailed across the Atlantic. This was done to save time and safeguard the delicate scientific equipment aboard *Hercules*. A 400-meter ship can travel much faster and more easily across the Atlantic than a 37-meter research vessel can.

R/V Hercules

I join Jeff in the lab. His research is complete, and we are ready to put his hypothesis, as to where the *Santisima* is, to the test. Expeditions are big, expensive tests! He shows me where he thinks the *Santisima* is on the map. We draw a big box around the area since we do not know the exact location where the ship sunk – that would be too easy. We start our search where we think it might be and hope that that's where it is. Like your backpack – you start looking where you think it is. One thing for sure is that if you find it – it's in the last place you look.

I plot the block on a nautical chart on the computer and fill it in with parallel lines. The lines overlain on the nautical chart show where we will be surveying; collecting sonar data in order to 'see' the seafloor. A nautical chart is similar to a topographical map – think Google Earth – only a nautical chart gives information about water, not land. It shows how deep the water is and identifies any seafloor hazards that we need to avoid. It is not good for a boat to hit a big rock or run into very shallow water. We are looking for shipwrecks – we don't want to become one.

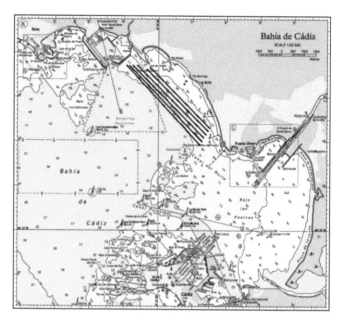

Nautical chart of Cadiz, Spain with survey block overlain

We discuss and strategize the best ways to conduct the upcoming survey. We are in uncharted waters, for although multibeam sonar has been in use since the 1960s, it has rarely been used for nautical archaeology. We will be one of the first to use it for this purpose.

Chapter 6

Ship Shape

Captain Dave is on the bridge looking at the chart on the now working monitor. He's a little grumpy. He's hungry, and I interrupt him on his way to lunch. King, our cook, prepared a feast – roast beef, mashed potatoes, and peas and carrots. There are ice cream bars for dessert. It's like Christmas. "I want to review the survey plan with you before we set sail tomorrow," I say.

He says, "Let's have a look."

We are not actually setting a sail, that's just a nautical expression for leaving the dock, whether it be a motor boat or a sail boat. Tomorrow will be the first day of the survey. *Hercules* is in tip-top condition, computers tested, multibeam, side scan, and ROV all calibrated, tested and ready to go. The weather is supposed to be good all week, so it is fortunate that we fixed the monitor quickly.

Good weather conditions are very important for surveying. The water must be calm, so the boat can stay on track and not be thrown off course. If either the wind or the waves are too strong, then the boat will bounce around like a floating top, unable to maintain a straight line.

Staying on a survey line is harder than you think. In your mind's eye draw a line in the water, now imagine driving a boat on that line. It is not easy. Additionally, the boat must drive very slowly so the data can be the very best it can be. If the water is choppy, the data will be choppy too.

Besides good weather being important for the data, it's also important for the people on board. It is not pleasant getting seasick. Big waves and strong winds are the perfect combination for a barf sandwich. Amazingly, I have never gotten sick, but have seen all the different colors people turn when they're getting sick. It's like seeing a rainbow go across someone's face but not in a good way. I can unequivocally – that means for sure – tell you that the end of the rainbow does not always lead to a pot of gold.

Chapter 7

Target Practice

It is now May 23rd. We have been surveying for two weeks. The two-hour route to the survey area is a well-worn path from the dock. We have collected gigabytes of data and so far have seen nothing that resembles a shipwreck. Our hopes are high; maybe today will be the day we find the *Santisima*. That is the best part of this job – you just never know when you will find something wonderful. Every day is a new day filled with promise.

It is 6 a.m. and we are pulling off the dock. Dave informs the boat crew to ready the boat to sail. Logan, John, and Gerry check the lines and anchors and secure any loose tools and equipment on deck. Bob, the engineer, starts the engines. The low hum of the engine vibrates throughout the vessel. *Hercules* comes to life with a burst of activity. Scientists and crew alike are all eager to begin the search for the *Santisima*. King is rushing around the galley as he begins to prepare breakfast. Yum, smells like chocolate chip pancakes.

It's a beautiful day. The sun is shining. The weather is hot. The water is sparkling like someone keeping a secret that they can't wait to give up. We pull off the dock and head out. As we cut through the calm water, dolphins join us off the bow enjoying a free ride on the crest of our wake.

Dolphins join the expedition

From the bridge the captain keeps watch for passing boats and fishermen. I begin the day's log with information detailing the date, time, position in latitude/longitude, speed, weather conditions, direction, and equipment settings. All this information will be important when we process the data.

There are many challenges as we prepare for the day. A typical survey day starts out by leaving dock by 6:00 a.m. and ferrying to the survey area. Ferry is a nautical term that means to travel a fixed route by a boat or plane. We survey for as long as the weather permits – usually eight to ten hours. At the end of the day we ferry back to the dock. The crew ties up to the dock and cleans the deck. King makes dinner. Michelle and I begin to back-up the day's data. We work late into the night.

The next morning, I was up at 5:00 a.m. as usual. I turned the multibeam on when we left the dock to 'warm it up' and ensure it's working perfectly before we get to the survey block. The survey block is the group of lines that we drive over back and forth, collecting data all along the way. As we 'drive' the lines, we create a map of the bottom of the sea from the data collected. Each day we have an ever-enlarging map of the seafloor.

I grab a second cup of coffee from the galley, which is what you call the kitchen on a boat, and head to the lab. It has been a long day already and its only 8:00 a.m. An hour later, we arrive at the survey area. I radio Dave on the intercom and let him know that we are ready to begin the first line of the day. Today, I monitor the multibeam and collect new data while Michelle processes yesterday's data. As Michelle processes the data, she looks for 'targets,' features that looks different than the surrounding area.

This may sound silly – definitely sounds silly, but the way I think of finding targets in multibeam data is from the *Sesame Street* song '*One of These Things*.' The first two lines of the song are, "One of these things is not like the others, one of these things doesn't belong." This is exactly what we are looking for. Something that doesn't belong.

I bet you are now humming '*One of These Things*' if you know it. Believe me, I had it stuck in my head more than once.

Target selecting from multibeam data

If you are in a very sandy area and all around is flat sand, then you see a big mound or sharp jagged edge, it's different, it doesn't belong. This is a target. Remember, every meter of the survey block is possibly where we'll find the *Santisima,* so we review the data with a fine-tooth comb. We carefully pick and reject targets based on size, location, look, and a bit of intuition. Over the last two weeks, we've improved and developed a target detecting technique. We continue to develop and fine-tune the process as the survey continues.

Finding a ship at the bottom of the ocean is like the old adage, 'finding a needle in a haystack.' If it were easy, everyone would do it.

Chapter 8

All Systems Go

We are collecting sonar data which gives us information about what's underneath the boat on the seafloor. We have two different sonar systems on *Hercules* – a side scan sonar and a multibeam sonar. Each sonar system is made up of several parts: a sonar, an operator station, a bridge display, a processing unit, and a data storage computer. It takes hundreds of meters of cables and wiring and a bit of luck to get all the bits and pieces working.

SONAR is an acronym and stands for **SO**und **N**avigation **A**nd **R**anging. A sonar detects objects under water by emitting sound pulses and detecting or measuring the return signal after being reflected. Whew, that's a mouthful! What does this all mean?

It means this:

Let's discuss the multibeam since we primarily used the multibeam for this cruise.

On the *Hercules* the sonar head of the multibeam is installed through a hole in the bottom of the boat called the moon pool. The operator station, processing unit, and data storage computer are in the lab and the bridge display, on the bridge.

A multibeam works by sending sound waves – multiple beams – 254 to be exact – from the sonar head down through the water column. Sound waves 'bounce' off the bottom and travel back up. The sonar head receives the return signal and records the time and intensity (strength) of the return wave. A lot of information is calculated from the return signal using **A LOT** of math.

Sonar Head

Sound waves transmitted to the seafloor, 'bounce' off the bottom and retun.

Map of the Seaflooor

Multibeam sonar uses sound waves to map the seafloor

A. Water Depth

One measurement that is calculated from the data collected from the multibeam is water depth. Although sophisticated mathematical operations are used, it is always important to understand the concept behind the calculations. You should always be able to tell if your results make sense.

To calculate water depth, we measure how long it takes for a sound wave to travel from the boat to the seafloor and multiply by the speed of sound through water. It takes four steps.

1) Record clock time the sound wave left the boat. Record clock time sound wave returned to boat.

2) Take the difference between the two clock times. This gives you the amount of time (units of time, t) that it took for the sound wave to go down and back.

3) Divide by 2. We divide by 2 because the wave went down to the bottom and back. You only want the time it took to go to the bottom.

4) Multiply by the speed of sound through water (units of distance over time, d/t). This gives you the final answer in distance. This is the distance from the boat to the bottom, in other words, water depth.

Remember in math, always mind your units. Let's try an example:

1) Record
Time wave left sonar 12:00:10.0 a.m.
Time wave return to sonar 12:00:10.5 a.m.

2) Subtract
The difference between the two times gives the amount of time it took for the wave to travel down and up.
12:00:10.5 a.m. – 12:00:10.0 a.m.   =   0.5 s

3) Divide
Time for sound to go down and up (t, time in seconds, s) divided by 2.
0.5 seconds / 2   =   0.25 s

4) Multiply
Speed of Sound through water (d/t, distance over time in meters/second, m/s) accepted estimate is 1,500 m/s
Water Depth =
0.25 seconds * 1500 meters/second   =   375 meters

Sound travels incredibly fast through water. 1,500 m/s equals 3,355 mph (miles per hour). Imagine that. It is a clunky, ramshackle car compared to the speed of light though. The speed of light is 299,792,458 m/s or 670,616,629 miles per hour.

B. Acoustic Reflectivity

The multibeam also collects the intensity of the return signal. Intensity is another word for strength. Acoustic reflectivity is a fancy term which means how much an object reflects sound. Think about it like this. Think of walking in mud and sand. When you step in dark, soft, gooey mud what happens? Your foot sinks in; it takes some effort and time to pull it out. Now think of what happens when you step on a white sandy beach. You can pick up your foot easily.

Imagine your feet are sound waves. The time and strength it takes for your foot to come out (return) from stepping in the mud is much greater than it is when picking your foot up from a sandy beach. It takes a lot to get your foot out of the mud! Mud absorbs more of the wave (your foot) than sand does. Another way of saying this is that sand is more reflective than mud.

Chapter 9

Bottoms Up

Now let's take acoustic reflectivity a step further and think about the seafloor, and how it can help us find the *Santisima*.

The substrate – what's on the bottom of the seafloor – is made up of mud, sand, shells, rocks, seaweed, wooden boats, and anchors and on and on and on – think of all the things you have stepped on in the water. All these different substrates have different return signals called signatures. Mud has a different signature than sand which has a different signature than rocks which has a different signature than shells et cetera, et cetera. You get the picture.

A backscatter map is generated from these returns, giving information which helps identify the bottom as rocks, sand, or mud to name a few. Anchors and wooden boats also have their own signatures and show up on the map as well. Backscatter imagery is particularly useful when selecting targets.

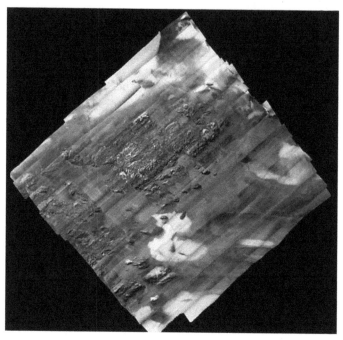

Backscatter imagery from multibeam, showing different substrate signatures

Another type of map we generate from the multibeam data is depth. The water is deep where we are surveying so it takes longer to collect quality data. The deeper the water the longer it takes for the signal to reach the bottom and return – transmitted and received. Why?

It takes time for the sound wave to travel from the sonar head to the sea floor and back. It's like the difference between running a 50-meter relay versus 100-meter relay. 50 meters is a shorter distance so takes less time. The return signal is the data we are collecting.

Now, add to this the fact that the boat is moving forward. Sound waves are traveling down and up as the boat is moving forward. Can you see this in your mind's eye? Picture yourself dribbling a basketball down the court. The ball is going up and down and you are traveling forward. The ball is the sound waves and you are the boat.

Ship's course moving forward

Sound waves transmitted through water column Water Column

Seafloor

Survey vessel moving forward collecting multibeam data as sound waves are transmitted and received

Now, if you want to have the ball bounce as much as possible as you move from one end of the court to the other what can you do to do that? The first thing you may think of is to dribble faster. That's a very good thought, but that won't work in this case. It won't work because we cannot change the speed of sound. It is a constant and we are not superheroes.

What is another way to have the ball bounce more as you run from one end of the court to the other? Did you think of something? Yes? The other way to have more bounces is to run slower – walk even. Can you see it? Go try it out and see for yourself.

So, in order to collect denser data – allowing more sound waves to travel down and back – we drive very slowly. The denser the data is – the more bounces you have running across court – the higher the resolution, the better the picture. It's the difference between watching an HD – High Definition, versus regular TV. You see a better picture on the TV that has the highest resolution. For finding shipwrecks, we found that we must drive as slow as possible, so the data is as sharp as possible.

Speaking of data, while processing yesterday's data Michelle shouts out, "I've found something!" We are very excited as to what it may be. I run to find Jeff.

Chapter 10

Sounds Like a Shipwreck

The data shows a bit of a mound in an otherwise very flat bottom. This is the trick to finding shipwrecks. Finding something that doesn't belong. When you look at the images, you look for something that's different.

Shells and rocks and sand have a natural flow. They may be smooth and have a pattern in their location. They all go together in a way that looks 'right.' Anthropogenic, human-made, objects look different than what is naturally occurring. When a ship drops to the bottom of the sea, it doesn't actually belong there.

Boats may have sharp edges and points depending how long they have been underwater. The longer something has been under water, the more it starts to become part of the natural habitat. I'm sure you've seen movies where cities are abandoned and reclaimed by nature. It's like that, only under water. A newer shipwreck made of metal which has not yet eroded is easier to detect than a wooden ship that has been under water for over 200 years and deteriorated over time.

Example of newer ship driven aground in 1971

We all gather around the monitor to have a better look at what Michelle found. She zooms in on the mound and uses a measuring tool to note the size and dimensions of the mound in the logbook. It measures 50 meters by 30 meters and is approximately 25 meters high on one end. It is oval shaped, one end sticking up slightly higher than the other which is quite encouraging.

When a ship capsizes, it rarely sinks straight to the bottom. And with a muddy bottom it makes sense that part of it sank deeper into the mud than the other. One end of the boat may be heavier where the anchors are kept. Anchors from the ships of that time were very heavy, weighing over 1,000 lbs.

We are looking at a small mound in a very smooth bottom with nothing around it, it could very well just be a small mound – nothing special. Or… it could be a piece of the *Santisima*. Jeff is in the lounge meticulously going through the 'Book of Targets.' I crab-walk my chair to the door heading into the lounge and yell, "Hey Jeff, we've found a really good target." We had to take the wheels off the chairs because when the boat rolls, so did the chairs. It was fun, but not for long. Jeff gets up and comes to see what we are looking at. After some discussion, he decides that further investigation is warranted. Or more easily put, it's worth a look.

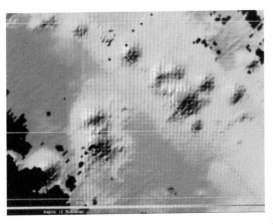

Processed multibeam data shows mounds on the seafloor

There is a delicious aroma wafting into the lab from the galley. King must be cooking up a special treat for lunch. Yes indeed, today is sizing up to be a good day.

Chapter 11

Rough Day at Work

I rolled out of my bunk this morning, literally. The harbor is rough, and *Hercules* is ROCKING, and I don't mean music. I try to brush my teeth and stab myself in the face with my toothbrush. The sink is right next to the bunkbeds in the cabin, which is the size of a closet. I can actually wash my face without getting out of bed.

I head upstairs grasping the handrails with both hands to keep my balance. King has the guardrails up on the stove, so the pots don't go flying off. He is not making anything fancy for breakfast, just cereal and toast, it's too dangerous to have an open flame. Besides no one's stomach wants a big meal on a pitching boat. I hobble to the coffee pot and only take ½ cup because any more than that would slosh out.

Michelle's already in the lab making sure that all the computers are secure. A mouse goes flying off the desk. Logbooks, pens, and external hard drives all become potential weapons of mass destruction as *Hercules* rocks and rolls. Above the wind, I hear the screech of the ropes securing *Hercules* to the dock as they rub against the rusty pier.

After battening down the lab, we head to the back deck to help Gerry, Logan and John put away any stray bits that are lying around. I grab a lounge chair as it slides towards the stern. We finish up. There will be no surveying today. It is too rough.

I go back to the lab. It is pointless to try to process yesterday's data. The screen is bouncing up and down in front of me, typing is impossible. My fingers have trouble connecting with the keyboard as the boat rocks forward and aft.

Processing is out. Even starting a data backup is not possible. With every lurch the computer drives can jump, which can damage or break the computer or worse – lose or corrupt data that we have already collected.

There is no other choice but to get off the boat and have a field trip. Dave and Bob stay behind on *Hercules*. We climb up the ladder to the pier. Standing on a non-moving substrate feels funny and my legs are wobbly. I think this may be where the expression of 'walking like a drunken sailor' comes from. We get in the van and head towards the city plaza. Gerry and King drop us at the city plaza, and head towards the supermarket to restock the galley with meat, vegies, salad, and Gummy Bears, Michelle's favorite.

John, Michelle, Logan, and I meet up with the archeologists from the Centre D'archéologie. They offer to give us a tour of the Centre and we spend the day at the museum and walking around the city of Cadiz. It is a rare treat to be off the boat and we thoroughly enjoy our time ashore.

Centre D'archéologie, Cadiz

In the afternoon we head back to *Hercules*. The weather has improved so we are able to run backups. We do a system check to make sure nothing broke during the day. Rocking boats wreak havoc on computers.

The archeologists have invited us out for dinner. In Spain, they eat dinner later than we eat on the boat. We have set meal times on *Hercules*; 8:00 a.m. – breakfast, 12:00 p.m. – lunch and 6:00 p.m. – dinner. No exceptions. Sunday afternoon we are on our own, King has the afternoon off. In between meals you can usually find him fishing off the back deck with a homemade fishing pole. I never actually saw him catch a fish until we got to Malta, but that's another story.

We head back into town at 9:00 p.m. for dinner, which is still early for dinner here, restaurants are just opening. We join Ana and the other archeologists at a dimly lit stone café on a cobbled road nestled between timeworn buildings. They order for us – and we savor the beautifully decorated dishes of cheese, jamón, olives, fish, and bread that look as good as they taste. As the evening continues, plates of tapas and pitchers of sangria crowd the table.

Tapas

Ana has a surprise for us. We look towards the small stage towards the back of the restaurant where two musicians are setting up drums. The guitar player sits on a small stool. Two women elaborately dressed in bright, almost florescent dresses whoosh past our table, the train of their dresses snap as they go by. Flamenco dancers!

We watch as the women begin to dance, stamping their feet, slowly at first, then increasing with speed and intensity as the musicians play faster and faster. The dancers play castanets, a pair of small wooden clappers held in each hand. The loud crack of the castanets is in unison with the stamp of their feet. It is a marvel to watch.

Flamenco Dancers

The surprise isn't over. Ana is friends with one of the dancers and during a break, they come to our table and offer to teach us how to dance the Flamenco. Although some of us are quite used to stamping our feet, putting it to music isn't so simple. When Logan stepped on John's foot who sent Michelle flying, we realized we were in a hazardous situation and we better stick to science. We gave Ana and her team a big hug, thanked them for their hospitality and headed back to the boat.

Chapter 12

Rover the ROV

Today is the day. The weather is better. Good enough to give it a go. Jeff selected the best targets based on location, depth, look, and size and we are going to investigate them further.

The water in the survey area is 90-meters deep and very rough and murky. Ninety meters is too deep and dangerous for the dive team to investigate. The deepest the divers can go is 60 meters – and at that depth they would not be able to stay down long. We decide to deploy Rover, our **R**emotely **O**perated **V**ehicle, ROV for short. Rover is equipped with a multibeam, video camera, manipulator arms, and lights.

A very long, strong, waterproof cable attached to the back of the ROV runs across the deck, through the galley and then attaches to a computer in the lab. This cable is called an umbilical and contains dozens of thin, delicate wires, some are even made of glass. If even one of these wires break, it could mean that Rover won't work, so we must be very careful when working with Rover. He is very temperamental.

Final checks on Rover

Everyone is scurrying about, focused on putting Rover in the water. Putting a robot in the water is not easy. It takes a lot of preparation and teamwork to get everything right. First, Captain Dave conducts a safety review. Safety always comes first, especially aboard a boat and around large, heavy equipment.

Dave reviews the PPE – Personal Protective Equipment – which includes safety vests, shoes with steel toes, hard hats, harnesses, and sometimes flashlights if you're working on the deck at night. He goes over who will oversee what equipment during deck operations; who will run the winch, who will handle the leads to the ROV, and who will handle the umbilical.

Once everyone knows their tasks for deployment, recovery procedures are discussed in detail, so everyone is well prepared and knows their job. We don't want any surprises. Surprises during deck operations can get equipment broken, or worse, people hurt. My dad, an avid scuba diver, always used to say, "Plan your dive and dive your plan." I have heeded his wise words all my life.

In the lab, there is also a lot to do. We check the cables from Rover to the lab and make sure that all the connections are working. We turn on the video. John stands on deck, smiles a goofy smile and waves into the camera. We see him on the monitor in the lab. I smile, "Great! The video is working." Now to test the manipulator arms. The arms are controlled by a control box in the lab, very much like an Xbox controller only much bigger and... it's REAL. We test the arms by putting a soda can on deck. Howard, the ROV pilot, uses the control box to maneuver the arms and picks up the can on the first try. Next, we test the thrusters which power and steer the ROV – like a gas pedal on a car and lights to see where we are going – it's dark 90 meters down.

Finally, we are ready to go.

Everyone has one last cookie before donning safety vests and hard hats. Howard, Michelle, and I stay in the lab to monitor the controls. Dave is on the bridge overseeing the launch and holding the *Hercules* steady. Logan, John, and Gerry are on the back deck doing final checks. Jeff is in the lounge and King is in the galley washing dishes. We use walkie talkies to stay in communication with each other and coordinate each step of the operation. *Hercules* is anchored close to the location of the target. Fingers crossed for the *Santisima*!

Logan and Gerry hook metal chains onto the ROV and attach them to the winch. John is operating the winch. Dave radios down an 'All Clear.' John and Gerry watch Logan at the winch. Ropes, called leads, are tied to the ROV. John and Gerry 'lead' Rover, suspended in midair, making sure it doesn't swing into anything. The winch lifts the 500-pound ROV higher and higher off the deck, high enough to clear the side of the boat. Logan gives John a signal and watches as Rover swings over the side of the *Hercules* and gently drops into the water. Splash down.

Deploying the ROV

Chapter 13

Ninety Meters Down

Rover is in the water. Howard puts his cup of coffee in the galley and returns to the lab. He takes the ROV controls. He uses both hands to maneuver Rover deeper and deeper down to the seafloor. One control is for steering right and left and the other is for going up and down. Strong bottom currents make it difficult to for the ROV to descend evenly. It is lurching back and forth, up and down.

Strong, bottom currents also make the water turbulent. Turbulent is another word for rough. These fast currents, water moving close to the bottom, are mixing up the mud making the water very cloudy. You can test this out by putting some fine dirt in a bottle of water and spinning it around. Be sure to close the top first.

As Rover approaches the seafloor, the bottom is hard to find because it is so murky. It looks like pea soup on the video monitor.

Screen shot from Rover's video

There is a big POOF of muddy water on the screen as Rover hits the bottom with a THUMP! On the video monitor, we watch the umbilical cable wave around in danger of getting tangled. Howard is quick to move the levers to drive Rover upwards, not too fast though, because going too fast may strain the quickly tangling cable. He steers the ROV forward so the cable gets behind the ROV. Good. Crisis averted. Whew, that was close, too close.

After a minute or two, the ROV reaches the location of the mound we found in the data. Howard drives Rover slowly back and forth over the location. The stirred-up bottom is making it very hard to see and he doesn't want to bump into anything, especially not the side of a shipwreck!

All that we can see on the screen in the lab is brown muddy water and a few fish streaking by here and there. The fish look very surprised at the sight of a great big yellow fish with a great big yellow tail with great big shiny eyes swimming after them, which is what Rover looks like to them I suppose.

Logan, John, and Gerry are on the back deck keeping watch of the cables and umbilical. Dave is holding *Hercules* steady which is getting tough as the wind and the waves are starting to build up. White caps are starting to form, and the waves are starting to grow. *Hercules* has begun to rock back and forth, pitching and rolling. The rocking is making me feel funny, my stomach is gurgling, I should not have had that second cookie.

Dave calls down and tells us we have to bring Rover up. We are disappointed but don't want to risk anymore bottom-time. The weather is getting worse; we see the dark clouds coming in from the east and it will take about a half an hour for the ROV to return to the surface. We must hurry before the clouds get any closer.

The ROV is underwater 90 meters down, about the size of a football field standing up. Howard steadies Rover and begins the ascent, deftly moving the vertical and horizontal controls to bring Rover to the surface.

Forty minutes later, Rover is safely back on deck, washed off and secured. The cables are unhooked, all the data copied and saved on the lab computers. Just in time! The dark clouds boil above us and it has started to rain – HARD! Everyone races to the galley for some hot chocolate that King has prepared.

We head into port and get ready for a new day.

Chapter 14

Bittersweet Isn't Only Chocolate

Over the month-long expedition, we found dozens of mounds using the multibeam data in the vicinity Jeff and the team of Spanish archeologists thought the *Santisima* and *Argonauta* were.

We collected hundreds of targets using the new techniques and procedures we developed. Using only multibeam sonar for nautical archeological expeditions was not widespread prior to this expedition. There was no documentation or 'how-to' book. With trial and error, using scientific method, we got better. We improved and developed ways to find shipwrecks using a multibeam sonar system. By fine-tuning settings, we established a methodology for processing and gridding data to obtain the best results.

We deployed the ROV several times on several targets over the course of the campaign. The scuba team dove on targets located in shallower water. We never were able to have the dive team dive on the deeper targets because the deep water, poor visibility, and strong currents made it unsafe. Remember the rule – safety first.

From the ROV data, all the targets were covered in fine silty mud, the thrusters on the ROV creating a poof of muddy water every time it neared the bottom. We were unable to take any good pictures due to the muddy water, so we were never able to confirm what the mounds in the multibeam data definitively were. That means, for sure.

Without divers or visual proof from video, we were unable to ground-truth any of the targets found in the multibeam data. To ground-truth means to check the accuracy of data by means of in situ observations. In other words, prove it. We could never confirm that the mounds we found were part of the *Santisima* as we were unable to take a sample. Without ground-truthing, either visually by divers or from video from the ROV, it is impossible to say for certain what we found. In science, it is essential to have proof.

We also learned that the area where we were surveying, where the *Santisima* was scuttled was where countless ships had wrecked. And it was also a place where local fishermen scuttle broken-down, out of commission boats – it was kind of like a ship graveyard. In my estimation, we didn't just find one shipwreck, we found heaps of them!

In particular, we found two mounds that were the correct size, shape, and location, to possibly be the *Santisima* or *Argonauta*. However, without physical proof we cannot say conclusively, that means for sure, that it was or wasn't them. The mysteries of the *Santisima* remain under the sea for now.

Although we were unable to prove that we discovered the *Santisima*, we 'discovered' how to successfully use multibeam sonar to find shipwrecks, developed techniques and methodologies that we will use on future expeditions to much success. We improved our techniques and developed better ways to conduct surveys. This is what science is all about. You learn, you experiment, and you develop new ways to achieve your goal.

Looking for shipwrecks is like that. Some days the weather is good, some days rough. On good days, you get up and go. Seek what it is you're looking for. On rough days, you stomp your feet and dance.

Chapter 15

Straight for the Strait

The expedition is over. We untie the lines and push away from the dock at Port Du Cadiz for the last time. Ana and the other archeologists wave goodbye as the *Hercules* sets sail. Our course is set for the Strait of Gibraltar, as was the *Santisima* hundreds of years ago.

We are prepared and ready for our next expedition. We leave Cadiz with a fond *adios*, enthusiastic to try out our new techniques and create new ones. There are more shipwrecks to be discovered. (According to Popular Science magazine, less than 1% of the world's shipwrecks have been explored). Imagine, the *Santa Maria*, one of the three ships brought to America by Christopher Columbus, in 1492, was never found, and still believed to be on the floor of the Caribbean Sea, somewhere off the coast of Haiti.

Will you be the explorer to find the *Santa Maria*?

Sitting in the galley, I ask Jeff what's next? Jeff smiles a sly smile and tells us a story about a fisherman who pulled up a bronze arm in his net off the coast of Italy. The arm was later found to be a piece of a Riace Bronze, one of two full-size Greek bronze statues of naked bearded warriors, made in about 460–450 BC.

You think shipwrecks are hard to find – how about a bronze statue missing an arm. I look across at Michelle, "We better test the magnetometers. I think we'll be needing them soon."

Survey's End

Bibliography

Mark Adkin, The Trafalgar Companion, 2005 Aurum Press
    Ltd., London, WC1B3AT
David Howarth, Trafalgar The Nelson Touch, 1969
    Kingsport Press In. Kingsport Tennessee
Roy Adkins, Nelson's Trafalgar Battle that Changed the
    World, 2004, Viking NY, NY
http://www.historyofwar.org/articles/battles_trafalgar2.ht
ml

Image Credits

Description	Credit
Vessel Blueprint	Robert Allen Naval Architects and Marine Engineers
Running Cables on a Boat	Emma Kerger, Contortionist at Pitt St Mall
Historical Document	https://picryl.com/media/manuscript-from-historic-memoirs-of-ireland-comprising-secret-records-of-the-866b2a
World West Indies / Cape Trafalgar	Content is the intellectual property of Esri and is used herein with permission. Copyright © 2020 Esri and its licensors. All rights reserved.
Strait of Gibraltar	Content is the intellectual property of Esri and is used herein with permission. Copyright © 2020 Esri and its licensors. All rights reserved.
Battle of Trafalgar	https://commons.wikimedia.org/wiki/File:Battle_Of_Trafalgar_By_William_Lionel_Wyllie,_Juno_Tower,_CFB_Halifax_Nova_Scotia.jpg
Hercules	RPM Nautical Foundation

Survey Lines, nautical chart of Cadiz	Imray Laurie Norie & Wilson Ltd, Wych House, The Broadway, St Ives, Cambridgeshire PE27 5BT, England
Dolphins	personal photo
Target	personal photo
multibeam	Property of NIWA LTD 2005 all rights reserved (reference 11-20859.tif).
backscatter	
sound waves	Property of NIWA LTD 2005 all rights reserved (reference 11-20859.tif).
shipwreck	EGS, High resolution bathymetric image of the SS Tiberia.
processed multibeam	
Centre D'archeologie	Copyright:Sergey Ashmarin, Information extracted from IPTC Photo Metadata
Tapas	https://www.pexels.com/@lina-kivaka-593836
Flamenco Dancer	Frankie Hatton
Final Checks on Rover	personal photo
Deploying the ROV	personal photo
Screen shot from ROV	Deep Ocean
Survey's end.	personal photo

Find out More

Boats and Water Craft
- Sea Scouts
  - https://seascout.org/

Cooking
- Sprouts Cooking Club
  - https://www.sproutscookingclub.org/about-us-main/

Marine Geology / Oceanography / Geomatics
- State University of New York Stony Brook
  - https://www.somas.stonybrook.edu/
- University of New Brunswick
- http://www.unb.ca/

Multibeam Sonars
- Center for Coastal and Ocean Mapping Joint Hydrographic Center
  - https://ccom.unh.edu/
- Cape Fear Community College Marine Technology
  - http://cfcc.edu/martech/marine-technology/

Nautical Archeology
- RPM Nautical Foundation
  - https://rpmnautical.org/
- Nautical Archaeology Society
  - https://www.nauticalarchaeologysociety.org/
- Texas A&M University
  - https://www.tamu.edu/

Remotely Operated Vehicles ROVs
- International ROV contest
  - https://www.marinetech.org/files/marine/files/ROV%20Competition/2018%20competition/Sponsors/ROVbro_2018_web.pdf
- MATE Marine Advanced Technology Education (MATE) Center
  - www.marinetech.org

SCUBA Diving
- Scuba Certification Agencies
  - https://www.leisurepro.com/blog/scuba-guides/scuba-certification-agencies-padi-naui-bsac-cmas-and-more/

The Expedition Team

The expedition team ashore for a day.

Me and Michelle

King

Dave

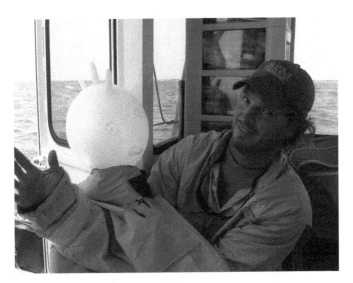

John

From left to right – Logan, Me, Jeff

Logan

Howard

CPSIA information can be obtained
at www.ICGtesting.com
Printed in the USA
LVHW050042230720
661004LV00027B/1088